King Charles III's Coronation

All rights reserved. No part of this publication may be reproduced, stored, distributed or transmitted in any form, by photocopy, recording or any other electronic-mechanical process, except in the case of brief quotations in critical texts, reviews and certain others, without the prior written permission of the publisher -commercial uses permitted by copyright law.

Royal Pageantry: The elaborate display of pomp and ceremony during the coronation, including colorful parades, military displays, and other traditional rituals.

State Banquet: A formal feast held in honor of the newly crowned monarch, attended by dignitaries and foreign diplomats, as part of the coronation celebrations.

King Charles III: The future monarch of the United Kingdom, who may undergo a coronation ceremony upon ascending to the throne, following the passing of the current monarch, Queen Elizabeth II.

Elizabeth II: Reigned as the Queen of the United Kingdom and other Commonwealth realms from 6 February 1952 until her passing in 2022. Throughout her lifetime, she held the position of queen regnant in 32 sovereign states and served as the head of state in 15 realms at the time of her demise.

Westminster Abbey: A historic church in London where most coronation ceremonies of British monarchs have taken place since 1066.

Coronation: The act or ceremony of crowning a monarch or sovereign, symbolizing their ascension to the throne.

United Kingdom:

A sovereign country comprising four countries, England, Scotland, Wales, and Northern Ireland, located off the northwestern coast of mainland Europe.

Acclamation: The formal announcement of the monarch's accession to the throne, usually made during the coronation ceremony.

Monarch: A sovereign ruler, such as a king or queen, who holds supreme authority over a kingdom or country.

King: The male ruler of a kingdom or realm, usually inheriting the title through birthright or by election.

Royal Family: The immediate family members of the reigning monarch, including the queen consort, prince consort, and their children.

Crown Jewels: A collection of precious gemstones, crowns, scepters, and other regalia used in the coronation ceremony to symbolize the monarchy's authority.

Archbishop of Canterbury: The senior bishop of the Church of England who traditionally presides over the coronation ceremony and crowns the monarch.

Procession: A ceremonial parade that takes place during the coronation, where the monarch travels from the royal residence to the coronation venue.

Sword of State: A ceremonial sword used in the coronation ceremony to symbolize the monarch's authority and power.

Orb: A symbolic globe carried by the monarch during the coronation ceremony, representing their sovereignty over the world.

Scepter: A ceremonial staff carried by the monarch during the coronation ceremony, symbolizing their authority and power.

Anointing: The act of applying sacred oil to the monarch's head during the coronation ceremony, signifying their consecration and blessing by God.

Homage: A ceremonial act where subjects pay respect and swear loyalty to the newly crowned monarch during the coronation ceremony.

Investiture: The act of bestowing the monarch with the symbols of their royal office, such as the crown, scepter, and orb, during the coronation ceremony.

Proclamation: The formal announcement of the monarch's accession to the throne, usually made during the coronation ceremony.

Printed in Great Britain
by Amazon